Planning My Escape

Mary Jo Homstad

━━ Springwater road ━━

Decorah, Iowa

2020

Published by
Springwater Road Publishing
3112 Springwater Road
Decorah, Iowa 52101

Copyright © 2020 by Carl Homstad

Most of the poems in this book were previously published in *Weavings* by Mary Jo Homstad (Bread & Butter Press, Denver, 1980), comprised of poems selected by Lucy Hanson Homstad following her daughter's death.

ISBN 978-0-57876-210-4

Cover design: Carl Homstad
Cover drawing: Mary Jo Homstad
Back cover photo: James Hockings

Printed in the United States of America

To Lucy Hanson Homstad

Contents

FOREWORD BY GREG BROWN   IX

INTRODUCTION   1

A SENSE OF PLACE   3

Iowa Countryside 3
Iowa Summer Poem 4
In Decorah Today 5
Decorah 6
dana 7
Farm Picnic 7
Canning Tomatoes 8
Smalltown, Iowa 10
Iowa Landscape 11
Conversation with John 12
Iowa 13
Leaving Home 14

LIFE'S LESSONS   15

How to Catch A Husband 15
To Katherine 16
Woman, thy womb 17
Just before Winter in Iowa 18
He is miserly with his words 18
Keosauqua 19
* Des Moines 20
Machine Shop Poem 20
Innocence 21
Departure 22
A Train Ride Across Russia 24
Traveling Through Russia 24
* Today, Junk Shops 25
Learning to Tell Time 26
Used-Book Store 30
"I remember ... " 30
Gossamer voices 31
I see dolphins 31
Mr. Golden and His Circus 32

* *Appearing in print for the first time.*

A Windy Day in Letts, Iowa 33
* Rain fingers the windows 34
* Profile of a Listener 35
The Guest 36

    LOVE AND FAMILY 37

How to Love a Turtle 37
Messages 38
You. 39
My voice cracked like ice 39
World Affairs 40
Unrequited Love 42
Fantasy 44
He who I thought 44
In the Field 45
I look at maps 46
Steel-toothed young handsome 46
A Lover Like Fall 47
Conversations with My Father 48
My Father 51
My Mother's Poem 52
A Birthday Poem 53
Lately when you walk through my mind 54

    CHILDREN 55

Promise 55
High school girls giggle 56
The evening wind blows 57
Lullaby 57
Thoughts on Children 58
poem 59
Twilight 60
To Mike 61
The boy put his head 62

    NATURE 63

I sleep outside 63
The cat eats a fly 64
Placid cows 64
Slaughter on the Highways 65
Fourth of July 66

* *Appearing in print for the first time.*

Refuge 67
Ode to Johanna 68
Moonlight, the swan 69
October Time of Night 70

THE LIFE OF A POET   71

A Poem to Storytellers Everywhere 71
* I seem to be waiting 72
i lie about my poetry 72
ever since the first word 73
One summer I was wedded to poetry 73
Writing Class: County Care Facility 74
A Skeleton of a Poem 75
To Mark 75
Crossing Spoon River in Illinois 75
* The Craft 76
* Oh, I have written enough sappy notes 77
Myths 78
We build our poems with lean speech 78
The Muse 79
No Place to Say 80
When One Can't Speak 80
Visiting Mr. Emerson's House at Concord 81
Four haiku 82
A Poem to Greg Brown 83
To Poet's Children 84
Ridicule 84
Tangled in the Sky 85
The Forming of a Poet 86

CONTEMPLATION   87

* A Moment 87
Make Straight the Way of the Lord 88
Prayer 89
Architects of the Universe 90
Shall I hit the fly 90
Old Poem 90
Being dreamers 90
I sense salvation in grey men 91
Second Week Alone, Tucson Desert 92

* *Appearing in print for the first time.*

"The monkey is reaching for the moon ..." 94
Come with me 94
Dark envelope of sleep 95
old woman 95
* Things move so fast 96
Jehovah Witness Visit 97
Source 97
Planning My Escape I 98
Planning My Escape II 99
Planning My Escape III 100
it is noon 102
The baby and Cosmo 102
Making Puppets 103
Chanting for My God 104
A Conversation 105
* Bizzy 105
* Why I Was Late 106

    MORTALITY   107

Death in the Iowa Winter 107
Self-portrait 108
Jock 110
Jock II 111
A Small Poem for Ralph 112
* Nursing Home Visit 113
Father William 114
Auction 116
Miss Brooks - 1977 116
Working at the Cafe 117
Cradles to Death 118
Clothes 126
Restaurant 126
To My Grandmother, Dying During a Snowstorm . . 127
The Gift 128
Weaving 129

    ACKNOWLEDGMENTS   CXXX

    ABOUT THE AUTHOR   CXXXI

* *Appearing in print for the first time.*

Foreword by Greg Brown

The daily is the holy. Mary was there, is here. Her poems are born in the holy and the daily flies out of them, tomatoes, old bodies, dust, family members. Everyone Mary wrote about was in her family. Everyone was welcome. Her poems slide easy as water.

Her ear is connected to her heart. Reading her poems I often laugh, I sometimes cry.

I see her there as plain as day. I say "Hello Mary. Thank you, thank you." I am so glad to see you again.

September, 2020

Introduction

Along with Mary's other siblings — my brothers James and Joseph — I decided that we should publish her work again, since the first poetry book *Weavings* was out of print. We decided that it should take a slightly different form. We wanted to concentrate on her poetry, because that was her life's work and greatest achievement. To that end, this second book has all the poems from the first, plus a dozen more, but leaves out the photos and drawings, with the exception of the cover. The poems are grouped by topic.

It is my hope that we have created a work that can appeal to poetry lovers beyond the circle of her friends and acquaintances, so she can receive the recognition as a poet that she so richly deserves.

Carl Homstad
Springwater, Iowa
October, 2020

A Sense of Place

Mary lived most of her adult life in rural Decorah, most of it in a farmhouse rented by a group of friends. Some of that group, including Mary, went together and bought the farmhouse and 40 acres in 1974. They built a community still known as Springwater Village.

Iowa Countryside
The perfect food

I eat the green rolling hills
Red barns and blue sky,
The bright sun slanting deliciously.

I eat it in huge great gulps,
Moving along harvesting all I see.

I eat it after a bonehard day
I eat knowing it is the perfect food
With its dancing light, green secrets
And dark vitality.

For dessert, I swallow clouds / lining and all.

Iowa Summer Poem

I walk down the leafy tunnel that leads to home
A cow
Fat and luxurious
Sits in my favorite pool,
And I shout down to her
This isn't India you know,
And she heaves her great bulk
Out of the pool
Looking at me with her soft eyes,
I walk on
A tiny speck
In the landscape
And all around me time flows.

In Decorah Today

People are dreaming at stoplights
Are they dreaming of stolen cats
perhaps a sacred stone left unturned
or their frog with the golden crown
left unfed?
It could be their thoughts wander
down alleys sipping bottles in brown paper
bags
Are they dreaming in kitchen-sink tones
or grey-flannel suit tones? Perhaps
they are coloring accusations in dull colors
Maybe they are imagining they are goldfish
sensuously moving their mouths to the rhythm
of water. Then again they could be burning
dinner
Or thinking "I should have said's" like little
smoke rings above their heads
The light changes; horns say their piece
and the dreamers move on
endless thought curving out behind

Decorah

The Norwegians held out their strong dreams
And sailed to a new world;

Digging in, they found good land
With hills like something native

They brought their brooding silences
Strong thoughts and worked the land

Populating it with blue-eyed children
And trolls that wandered off
To find their own reflections.

Here the winters still demand endurance
And still the strong silences remain;

Here one senses the trolls and nisse
Trading their faces for limestone bluffs,

Here the blue-eyed children look at these hills
And hum the tunes of waterfalls

And once a year, remember the source of
Their dream.

dana

> crystal eyes
> sparkle (earthly stars)
> laughing like water
> you swim easily through her mind.

Farm Picnic

> faces full like a well-turned jam
> smeared with raspberry happiness.

Canning Tomatoes

and all the world could be a tomato
for all i know
the trees are tomatoes and the road
the music is tomato music
and the bread is tomato bread
and the moon shines tomato red
and the dinner is tomatoes dressed in cheese
and so is my bed

i try to give things their due
tomato dance
my fingers are tomatoes
and my toes
and i try to respect the tomatoes
as the fine fruit they are

i try to cut with a painless ease
and yet my fingers
strangle   and tomato
blood
red and thin
pours out
into my pan   onto the floor
out of my eyes
and I am sticky with tomatoes
a tomato floor
i dance a tomato dance
and try to get my eyes to shine
but i am drowning
surrounded by totally uncaring
tomatoes

letting themselves be handled
this way and that
never protesting
squishing like good tomatoes should
ah tomato stew
what i would
or wouldn't do for you
what do i know of the world
but this tomato
scene
misted like some
strange dream
i think that i will love you 'til i die

and all these tomatoes do
is sit
and cannot even make me cry

Maggie says we call on God
when there is no return
for what we are sending out

Ah Lord,
are You a tomato
too?

Smalltown, Iowa

Religion on the coffee tables
swirling in the dust of silent streets;
religion in the refrigerator;
potato salad, fried chicken roast pig
catfish, three bean salad, corn...
All
Add to the weight of Iowa
raising the largest bellies
in the world. A practical people:
"We cash no checks from strangers"
They name their towns
Correctionville, Diagonal
The downtown buildings
age like sets in old westerns
They go to the city to shop

Iowa Landscape

You feel as if you
could be buried in
her fields & come
up alive & green -
Her colors harmonize
and sing in four parts
green / brown / gold / black
Her hills are nurture
and you long to call
her Mother
and lie atop her
sucking her soft energy
But she is also fierce
in those white days
that stretch between fall & spring
admonishing you to know your place -

Conversation with John

And I wanted to tell him why I was here.
To learn to be humble. To praise God.
To get my hungry finger into the soil. To learn
to concentrate. To finish a dream. To learn the
art of magic. To pull muscles
into survival leanness - And to let go -
And why shouldn't he.
All of us. Simply let go. I'll keep coming
back until I learn. And I look forward
to each day.

Iowa

Misted hills
like
some
ancient scroll
I take
a brush
and paint
a landscape
I
am
the
still
small
figure
going home

Leaving Home

I have made patterns here
In deep December snows
Hugging firewood to warm sleep.
Barefoot I have padded
Down icy stairs spying milk and cats
On the table thinking they are unseen.

I hear the dust settling
Like packing in a crate.
I have touched every dish
And washed them with every emotion.

I have been a part of subtle changes
Adding to a difficult whole.

I have slept late to the sound
Of frying eggs and cream being poured in coffee.
I have taken food from the land
Stored and brought out to delight paler times.

But something opens the door for me
(It cannot be the wind)   And it is time to

Move on, I pack the laughter and the stories
The music and the quarrels; whistling I put

Them all under my arm and move on down the road.

LIFE'S LESSONS

Mary was a keen observer of people. Many of her poems deal with advice she was given, and some that she gave. She had many close friends that were much older than she was.

How to Catch A Husband

*Advice given by a farmer's wife
in my 29th year*

To find a husband
Get out more
Go to church socials
Don't wait too long
Or be too choosy
You shouldn't wait for
Someone perfect
For you aren't, you know;
Get a cow.

To Katherine

> *- Long since dead*
> *and never met*

All day long I have written your name
In the dust of your past.

There are photographs of you studying in Paris
In your long skirt and haughty eyes.

Worldly ways in small town confines,
Katherine, how did you spend your nights?

With your starched virginity
Dim lit parlors and piano?

I hang your etching on my wall
And read your poetry with its precise longing.

I keep your parrot feathers in a box
And one aged photograph,

Of your father outside in the winter.

Woman, thy womb ...

Woman, thy womb
is of the sheltering
giving space.

How sound waves move
and how the engine works,

How to measure earth and sky
How to buy and How to sell,
The mechanics of this life on Earth
seem to be left to men

You measure things in heartbeats
and the warmth of skin.

Just before Winter in Iowa

The old man has taken
To roaring these days
Like restless sea;
He is ready to make
His appearance
He slaps his hands together
And stomps his feet
Laughing at our
Frail selves
Hiding in our small corners

He is miserly with his words ...

He is miserly with his words
        counting them out with long bony fingers
            They scrape the air like bone
                he has kept all the meat

Keosauqua

History runs through these streets
like a river
brightly-lit hotels echo riverboat captains
polish   step on wood
old fans
bay windows
quilts   and washstands - Brick houses
spaced a neighborly distance apart
laze quietly speaking in the Industriousness
of brick
practical people let grass and gardens
grow long between houses
and the beauty of the Presbyterian church
in cyprus grove
on a hill / is austere and simple
no fancy language for these pioneers.
Simple utility - when evening came it
brought a hush / & the dull glow of
kerosene / They kept boundaries
          & made good neighbors / and
          time was a light-hearted guest

* Des Moines

Men like things to do
houses to build
And campers.
I like things to build
like lives
and happiness.

Machine Shop Poem

The creator (bossman)
Views us as
extensions of his machines
if he saw the creator
in us
we could no longer do his work
we would see into each other's eyes . . . .

Innocence

Listen!
I am innocent. Completely.
    I am innocent
    I am.
I don't know why I go around
Feeling guilty
When I am innocent.

I confess my guilt
Before the crime.
    Afraid of my own innocence
    Afraid of not being guilty.
Which is strange.

And why I have a bad time in life,
Always apologizing for a crime
I am not going to commit.
    Afraid to confess my own innocence
    And surrender.
I have nothing to hide.
NOTHING TO HIDE.
    Because I am innocent.
    I am.

Departure

My cautious mouth looks the opposite way
And runs into a stream of traffic.
Talking a lot, the mind is run over by
A huge purple Cadillac.

And the driver never misses a beat.
I pick up my tongue
And move on.

I notice there is dust on my eyeballs
And I cannot read my fingers,

I know somewhere there is a place to get them clean;
By this time I am hanging on to sighs,

I am not desperate.
But my ears have taken to telling my nose what to do

And my stomach is playing a bass drum
In an orchestra out of town.

I tap my teeth with a silver icepick
And tell my mind to do something.

It is busy carrying on an amusing conversation
With itself.

> > >

I take the night freight out of town
And whisper to my hands to please not betray me.

I find that my knees are crossed
And that my bones have already passed judgment,

So there is nothing to do but stay on the train
And ride.

A Train Ride Across Russia

empty
minded
strained
drained
brain
into
countless
windows
passing
houses
telephone wires
straining
with
unheard
voices
And
unseen
faces
in
millions
of
windows

Traveling Through Russia

I wonder if my roots show.
i must look as if i were
freshly dug up.

* Today, Junk Shops

discarded
castoff
We go in search of something
to make ours
that has been somebody elses.
To regenerate with care
a coffee cup
replete with stains
from some morning or evening ritual.
Price $1.00.
I'll give it to you for 50 cents
he says.
I have 50 cents in my hand and it becomes automatic.
And it is mine
complete with coffee stains.
And so I begin yet another phase
holding my coffee cup with love for only love
will make it mine
and
Take away the forlorn
air.
We are capable through
care
of breathing life into every object
found
and thus build a life full
of spirit
of the things we love

Learning to Tell Time

Eight a.m.
> It is the hour of the dreamstealers, the hour of the fish, the hour that is hooked and brought flopping into the day
> It is an hour of beginnings and endings
> the hour of separation
> It is the eye in the needle hour

Nine
> It is the hour of the rooster
> It is the no turning back time, the time when the body is no longer declared dead
> It is the spring hour
> the hour of the diving board

Ten
> It is the hour with an eye in it
> It is the hour of the prairie
> the hour that can see for miles
> It is the hour for gathering
> It is the hour of the squirrel
> It is the hour that has all the maps

Eleven
> It is the hour that borders on a gate
> It is a watchtower hour
> the hour of the horse
> It is the hour that is just learning how to fly

> > > >

Noon
    Noon is a great favorite of the sun
    It is a July hour
    the hour with a gate in it
    the hour that exists for the sake of the
    other hours
    the hour of the pig

One p.m.
    The hour of the dreamer
    the hour that digests
    a sometimes lazy hour that leans on noon
    It is the hour that sometimes wishes it could
    trade places with another hour
    It is the beginning of the downhill hours
    It is the hour of the cat, cleaning, and
    stretching

Two
    The wonder-what-other-people-are-doing hour
    the hour with a window in it
    the hour which is the child in the middle
    of a big family
    the hour which doesn't always get heard
    the hour that sometimes gets bored

Three
    It is an earnest hour willing to try and
    please
    It is a late August hour
    the hour of anticipation
    It is an hour that has some ambition
    It is the hour of the goldfish

    > > >

Four
> It is the hour of the ant
> the hour that saves string
> It is the hour that starts rumors
> It is the hour that suffers from attacks of
> anxiety and reminds one of one's maiden aunt

Five
> It is an hour on hinges
> It is the hour that goes out the gate and
> crosses the bridge
> It is an hour that knows where it's going
> It is the hour of the wild geese

Six
> It is the father hour
> the hour of the magician putting back together
> that which has been apart
> It is an hour that sustains
> It is an hour that will always be loyal
> It is an hour that knows how to embrace
> The hour that is mortar
> The hour of the seamstress
> It is the hour of the dog

Seven
> It is the October hour
> the hour that the sun has heeded a call
> and left
> a floating hour
> the hour of the snail

Eight
> This hour is whatever you want it to be
> It is the free space on the board
> the blank letter in the Scrabble game
> the wild card.

> \> \> \>

Nine
> It is the hour when the cat wants to go out
> the watching of the killing of time hour
> the hour of the crocodile
> a dangerous hour for the restless

Ten
> It is a December hour
> the hour with a crack in it
> the empty street hour
> the hour of the lamp-post
> the hour that understands the language
> of the wind
> the hour in which trees begin their conversations
> with one another

Eleven
> It is a winter hour
> an hour that stares into the fire and says very little
> It is the hour of the searcher
> the restless
> the drunk
> It is the hour that gives gifts to lovers
> and solitude to scholars

Midnight
> It is the hour noon turned inside out
> It is the hour of the distant bell
> It is the hour that studies mysteries
> It is the hour that has a door in it
> The thin curtain between worlds
> The hour of revelry and strange music
> An hour of reckoning
> The hour of Pan.

Used-Book Store

I see abandoned books
waiting like dark Polish ladies
in train stations
I want to take them
all home, but I know they'll
remain heavy - filling my house
with their shopping bags
and black umbrellas.

"I remember ... "

"I remember a dance
I remember I wore white
I remember mama said
Be careful
And I wasn't."

Gossamer voices

Gossamer voices
spinning
spider-like thread
catching your mind
in things
not said

Grasping little whisperings
echoing down the halls
seen in eyes
and written on walls

Answer them not
stay out of webs
wings
are made for the skies

I see dolphins ...

I see dolphins surfacing again and again
bodies in moonlight
dried by palms of wind -
Gypsies carry fire and smoke blankets
making safe campfires
On the edge of small towns.

Mr. Golden and His Circus

Elephants ride in semis
Tigers are let out
To growl at the trainer's whip
Blonde ladies fly
Then take down the equipment
Knowing its every detail.
The circus comes apart
Before our eyes;

The rings break
Into sections
The trapeze
Fits into boxes
The lion tamer's cage
Collapses

The clowns enjoy a beer
Behind their trailers.

A Windy Day in Letts, Iowa

The wind blew like an old woman
sweeping dust furiously
and we were caught standing
outside her door
It blew like a gossip
who could talk for six hours straight
and never ask you if you want any tea
It blew like an insistent salesman
and you wanted to say, "Yes, yes,
I'll take anything, just calm down"
It whispered too loud a secret
you didn't want to know
It made us bow our heads like reeds
praying for calm to hear the stars

* Rain fingers the windows ...

Rain Fingers the windows.
I am tracing thoughts with
smoke.

This which we think
is solid
is water.

Monks sit in hooded habits
circumventing the world
in God.

Sailors sit on deck
dreaming of wind and oceans.

Engineers train circuits
to move in waves
entering the spiral of
hearings.

Artists move brushes
Inventing new landscapes.

Carpenters see dreams
and hammer reality.

* Profile of a Listener

He is blind.
He is a gentleman
of the old school.
With old world manners.
In his youth someone gave him a violin.

He is a musician.
Music fills his sight.
Music gives color and shape
to his world.

He is 76 years old
and lives alone and
has for the last
six years.

He is accustomed to taking
care of himself.
Music takes care
of him.

When he plays the violin
the sound is his sight.
And it reaches into
your heart.

The Guest

I showed the mirror to my guest
And she concurred it was time to leave
Her restlessness had stirred up piles of dust
And we were both embarrassed
My house was not in order
How could it be when she lolled around all day
Painted brazen colors
And uncovered hips that asked to tell your fortune
Like some carnival gypsy

I admit I had invited her in
One wet sensual day
When the moon was full
I had been reading stories with my fingers
Deep in the forest, naked in a pool

But I didn't think she would stay so long
Or make herself so much at home
After she agreed to leave (it must have been the mirror)
I tore down my red velvet curtains
And threw my fantasies out the opened window

Love and Family

Mary was what you would call a people person, and she had close friends of all ages. She was very close with her parents and three brothers. Although she never married, she had several romantic relationships.

How to Love a Turtle

   - to Larry

don't tell him you love him
make him warm
feed him
lie with him
cry with him
      (though turtles' tears are rare)
let him go into his shell
do not disturb him
      (he'll come out on his own)
give him time
don't let him get you down
don't need him
let him run alone
      (he likes it)

Messages

minds minding
but they are such
gentle, men
with eyes of
liquid secrets
i only want to be
a quiet exquisite
piece of art
So incredibly silent
and beautiful
that men,
gentle men fall in love
with me -
That i cause nothing,
nothing to happen
except love.

You.

How you rise from the past
    Dark and straightforward as sin
    your eyes, tales told by
    drowned sailors
    from a place
    smelling of broken slavery & bay rum
    Where twilight steals your intention
    & night offers no escape
        we would wrap ourselves in deep
        shadows
    And in the morning we rise as strangers.

My voice cracked like ice ...

My voice cracked like ice
You mistook it for weakness
i say it was temporary insanity.
The wind says nothing
and the mounts roar out their
silence
    and thus i am taught to be quiet.

World Affairs

Drunken martini soaked
country clubbed
smelling of olives and success
Another drink, sir
(falling eyelids belie)
and state senator speaks
on world affairs
and successful men
smelling of steak
listen
President Kennedy walked through
the rose garden in Vienna
and Khrushchev
but I only want
to walk through the garden
with you
World affairs, world explosion
and a billion slivers
(in i's)
of unseen, unfree
black crows
perched on riches and words

> > >

I withdraw to explore inside
a billion tiny universes
before the whole world explodes
Talk on
Drink
and drown in your words
Rising star,
my Japan
of crowded free
and sky
and me

I miss you

Unrequited Love

He danced into my eyes
But then all the signs said he would
And then they said no more.

I let him stay behind
My longing eyelids,
I should have let him go.

His dance has become the weight of time
And all my dreams are rivers.

I have wandered in tangled forests
Beating my breasts,
Like the women of Jerusalem.

Like a child
I pleaded with my Father
And like a preening adolescent,
I did not stay to hear His answer.

I followed the fingers of a poet,
Who painted the sunrise on my heart
With watercolor
And then it rained.

> > >

I returned
No heroine,
Moral teachings like sand running
Through my fingers.

He who yet wanders through my blood
Is striving to be an upright man
And has no wish to lie with me.

I must rid my mind of this confusion
And teach my eyes new melodies
And think no more of dancing.

Fantasy

In my fantasy
      i gracefully in complete control
      and as casually as a car accident

  walk out.   (on you)

He who I thought ...

He who I thought has a heart of stone
Let me beat against it
Until I had hammered out my own salvation.

In the Field

Backs bent in peasant poses
Bending over in rows of weeds
The new one next to me asks,
"Were you ever asked to marry?"

I answer, "Yes"
"Why didn't you?"

How could I say
The knee had a false bend
The proposal was brittle
Like a winter day?

There was no ring
But the hollow one of words

How could I tell
    The mocking shadow
    Hung around your head
    Made everything empty as wind.

How could I explain
That I laughed and said,
"You don't want to marry me
It's a mere formality, trait of guilt."

"It wasn't right," I say.
We go on working
In our uninterrupted rhythm.

I look at maps ...

I look at maps to see where
you are
But there are no lines, colors or symbols
to indicate the whereabouts of your heart.

Steel-toothed young handsome ...

Steel-toothed young handsome black-haired jewish boys
named Steve or somesuch, displaying egos like new bikes
Standing around shopping centers all over America
breaking hearts like mine

A Lover Like Fall

- to Doug

There should be room in every life
For something unspoken
Unfinished
Forever in the making,
A season like Fall
A time like twilight;
A secret that only happens
On the full summer moon.

Someone who once
Without touching
Made love to you
And leaves messages
Out of snowflakes
On your front door.

Conversations with My Father

My father and I drink Aquavit
Dreaming we are Norwegian peasants.

He explains the meaning of the weather:
"Air is no different than water," he says
Men are no different than the weather, I think.

He goes on,
Explaining atmospheric pressure; he says,
"When the barometer is down
more babies are dropped from their mothers' wombs."

I have visions of babies dropping like rain
And mothers crying tears of indifference.

He asks me if I know how much air is pushing down on us.
I want to say we are all under pressure,
But he answers,"Twenty-nine pounds per square inch."

Tell me
How many pounds per square inch of love
But I do not ask
Instead I lift my glass in toast to peasants everywhere.

> > >

"The atmospheric pressure gets greater as you go lower,"
He says.
Ah ha, that's why poets get the bends and some even explode,
I say to myself.

He goes on with facts,
And I really listen.
Then he says,
"You never accused me of being smart."
Ah, I think, here it is.

And I remember all my self-centered years
When he was like a fish,
Opening and closing his mouth underwater.

Here we share a cigar,
The Indians knew
And we too recognize a peace pipe when we see one.

Stories of the past rise up and walk.
"Back in the sloppy days," he says,
"we drank a lot of beer,
leaving wet circles on the table.
I thought a lot about those circles."
And here we are father and daughter

> > >

Skipping thoughts like stones,
Watching concentric circles of time.

Then his eyes were moving in waves,
And his hands were whispering way back.
"Ten-cent beer, dinner cost a quarter, smalltown,
yes, we were small-town nobodies."

The last word comes out like a chant and a moan,
Small-town nobody.
(Ambition must have bitten him in the cradle
like some summer insect)
I said whoever told him he was a nobody had been lying
And if he had told himself, he was a liar too.

He never admitted it was a lie,
And vowed to become somebody.
And did.

But who was left to celebrate?

My Father

We lived in his pockets
Until he became wise
And emptied them;
Then like hungry church mice
We climbed out
And discovered
His heart
Beating with
A deep
Irregular love.

Buried deep
In the folds of his coat
We hadn't heard
The gnawing
Of our greed;
Now we see
He is dying,
We could walk through
The holes in his heart.

My Mother's Poem

My mother brings fresh flowers
and dusts around my words

She pours clear water into my hands
and tries to teach me how to spell sacrafice

For her the vases of my hands will always
have fresh flowers
and all my poems, titles

A Birthday Poem

Dear Mother,

    So you too arrived out of a spiral
onto earth
    And learned to string the beads of
Love upon the thread of Life
    You grew and became a mother and
Demands were put upon you: Your time
    was children [messes, tears and laughter]
    Now as a grown woman I have forgotten
The daily incidents of childhood and your
    Daily reactions, but I have not
Forgotten the wisdom you knowingly
    Or unknowingly transfered to
Me, that I may learn to string
    The beads of Love upon the thread
Of Life.
    And today i celebrate in my heart
The day of birth of the one who
    Taught me what Love is!

    Happy Birthday

Lately when you walk through my mind . . .

Lately when you walk through my mind
there is a lonely wind that whistles down deep canyons

thin coyote cries
& barren caves,
abandoned towns

So I have learned to sense your coming
and shut the door
Lest what I see becomes as lonely
As what I feel when you walk through my mind.

Children

Mary was never married and didn't have children, but she loved to be with them and often taught and took care of them. In many ways she managed to keep a childlike quality herself.

Promise

The days have flown.
    I made promises to the moon
    That on the next clear night
    We would dance until dawn.
But I protest, Time goes too fast.
    Promises made to the moon
    Or children
    Are not soon forgotten.

High school girls giggle ...

High school girls giggle
Blowing blue smoke rings
Like Egyptian
Princesses.

I keep a vigil.
An old lamp
Keeps a small light.
I sit cross-legged
In this temple, smelling
Of late afternoons.
Of lemons and wood;
Waiting like Isis
For wings.

The evening wind blows ...

The evening wind blows
as Mark would say - feathers,
and time dusts its people off

Somewhere there are lives being led quietly
gracefully, with full devotion
like a mother
full of the
moon and child.

Lullaby

Goodnight sweet one
May luminous wings
Float through your dreams
And love be stilled in its flight.

May you wander in the deep lands
Of night
And the seeds planted there
Wake to the light;

Goodnight   goodnight

Thoughts on Children

Time's muddy dance
           stamping the weight of the earth
on my coffee stained eyelids
           and I swear I can stand no more!
Children,
You are monsters
We have broken off ourselves
To pinprick our souls
you bounce
On my taut

Weaknesses
Like a trampoline
And when I tell you to get off

You only laugh

You know what is good for me.

poem

when as
children
we posed
before mirrors
and
dreamed
in waves

how could
we know
it
would
come in a
flood
and we
would
have no way
to stop
it.

Twilight

Twilight is when children
Put on their long pointed hats
And become magicians
Putting everything under
Their spell
Changing themselves as well.
They become toads and ghosts
Robbers, Robin Hood
They are roads
Speeding cars
On their way to Mars
Fireflies in jars
Stars!

Twilight does not have
An adult voice
It breathes softly
And denies nothing.

To Mike

    When it was summer and you were two
    We harnessed up the mules at midnight
    And gathered hay.

Your father hung a lantern
On the wagon
And we danced a gathering-hay-at-midnight dance.

    When it was summer and you were two
    The mules snorted summer songs
    Do you remember?

The smell was the smell of sweet
Summer companionship,
There was a storm coming
We pitched the hay as fast as we could
Lightning and fireflies
Answering our joy.

    Do you remember?
    You were two
    And it was summer.

I only wrote this poem
So some day you could remember.
And because I love you.

The boy put his head ...

The boy put his head upon
the table - we were talking -
he put his head down.
We noticed.
We asked him if he
were tired.
He said his neck hurt.
We had of course
been ignoring him -
we caught it -
and let ourselves
let him shine -
& he did.

Nature

Living in the country provided Mary with a deep knowledge and appreciation for the natural world, and she loved gardening, hiking, and meditating outside.

I sleep outside ...

I sleep outside to let
fresh air
into my eyes.
I sleep in the garden
to let my dreams be about
growing.

The cat eats a fly ...

The cat eats a fly
and then
looks to see
where it has gone

Placid cows ...

Placid cows grazing
All that patience turns
To milk

Slaughter on the Highways

So many of them,
Kittens and badgers
Skunks and rabbits:
Guts spilled
Like a tipped-over grocery cart;

I try to imagine
The speed, the power . . . .
But then it is all over in a second.

Fourth of July

Natureless man
vomiting your
defeated celebration
on defenseless land

your identity is strewn
in tinfoil, old food and beer

you are what you leave
i hope we never meet.

Refuge

I should like a dress made of evening
trailing the humid buzz of an insect
Made of wings of diaphanous moths
singing of wheat bowing on moonlit nights
To a great partner / trailing dew
for the tracks of the thirsty
Spelling refuge
Marking the folds of the earth.

Ode to Johanna

You are ballet dance, tiger, lost child
and bloodthirsty innocence, you bring
inanimate things to life and leave your
calling card in every corner, you are
graciously vicious, coldly affectionate.
You are in deadly playfulness
like a sumo wrestler walking away as if
    disinterested
You object to being held only to get as
    close
as possible at night
You are convinced you are a tiger
(you are after all a walter mitty among
    cats)
sleeping dreams of jungles
and soft as the dawn...

Moonlight, the swan . . .

Moonlight, the swan in the gathering darkness
     me, with my passion for philosophy illustrations
     and the hours
     drifting, in love with illusion
     in a nest of mirrors
     some sorcery melts my words
     And I am left simple
     I even try to steal the songs of twilight
          silenced by their melancholy
     I hoe in my garden of lovers
     & take home a bouquet of simplicities.

October Time of Night

There is a time
In the evening,

When neither the day
Nor sleep
Possesses.

Tight-lipped houses
Stare like blue-haired
Ladies.

Demure rooms speak
Through parted
Curtains.

Brazen rooms
Wide open
Reveal

Sacred scenes;

A man smoking his pipe
Reads the news,

A straight-backed girl
Practices the piano,

A woman weaves yarn
Around her fingers.

It is the October time of night.

The Life of a Poet

Mary took her calling as a poet seriously, although it is not a lucrative career. She did spend time teaching poetry in nursing homes, schools, and on the Iowa Arts Council's Touring Arts Team. Other than that, she did a variety of jobs to pay the bills.

A Poem to Storytellers Everywhere

Ride witches wind high!
Speak Princes in frog voices!
Know the poverty of stones
you tomb-wise trolls
Magic peels the waves back
one by one
in the half-lit cave
of the ear;
Storyteller rescues us
from hollow moons
and stiff-necked clouds
naming stars and holy places.

* I seem to be waiting ...

I seem to be waiting for that
quiet evening of intense writing
When I am wide awake.
So wide awake my soul sings
and my pen flies
and the wind blows through the trees.
Lately I have much to say
but am ready for bed
and always I will write it down tomorrow.
This book is full of blank tomorrows
and sketchy yesterdays.

i lie about my poetry ...

i lie about my poetry
& say they are letters
stuffing them into pillows
for restless dreams

ever since the first word ...

ever since the first word
words have been putting on flesh;

poets, be cautious
you shall see your words
walk before the night is over.

One summer I was wedded to poetry ...

One summer I was wedded to poetry
My veil was black
and at the marriage ceremony
They played a funeral
March

Writing Class: County Care Facility

She was sitting there silent when her memory danced out taking words as garments and telling us of her loss, seed of her flesh, disappearing into the veil of night, silently as before the first word. Not a single cry, not a warning, or a wail of loss, just the child being taken to some other room beyond hearing. And a voice, telling but not explaining, leaving the room voiceless and a memory crystal as ice.

She was sitting
Silent in the corner.
We were talking about
Memory; she spoke -
The only thing she ever told us:

"That night I heard a voice,
'The baby is dead,' it said.
I woke up my husband and told him
'The baby is dead.'
He said 'Don't be foolish,
Go back to sleep.'
But I knew I had heard
We got up to look, and yes
The baby was dead."

She got up and left us.
We were quiet for a moment
then continued.

A Skeleton of a Poem

Most of it is just padding
To make us look fat,
When in reality
We are bare bones
Looking for a home.

To Mark

You know how those poets are
Strange as sin
staring into the round bowls of bingo parlours
making words out of smoke.

Crossing Spoon River in Illinois

I breathe ghosts
And feed them my thoughts
Together we cross Spoon River
And write my eulogy

* The Craft

My identity is not the Craft
but comes from way inside, the
Craft is what I must do
to achieve some relative wholeness.
To hammer out of this seemingly
incoherent life, some sense,
some reasoning.
I do not write to be a writer but to
participate fully in what is
called life.
It is not unlike fishing
gardening.
The skill
but it still takes something akin to luck
and patience to land anything.

* Oh, I have written enough sappy notes ...

Oh, I have written enough sappy notes.
Said uncentered things.
I go now to my center, slowly,
patiently inward to balance
to find the only solidarity I know.
I have no more words to say
no more words to write.
I inscribe a Huge white silence
and wrap it around me.

You whirl around
like a whirlwind I saw in the desert.
But I have stepped out
And remain unperturbed outside.
Balanced, and now silent.

Silent.

Myths

I am looking for a Myth that
hasn't been written.

I fill my huge Notebooks
with fine lines.

Waking up in the morning to discover
they have walked off the job.

I start again.
It is my job.

Bound like Prometheus
for thirty thousand years.

Every day my memory is lost
and every day returned.

Who will forgive me for stealing fire
from the gods?

We build our poems with lean speech ...

We build our poems with lean speech
And our elders complain there is no rhyme
(that waving, rocking speech, putting them
into easy sleep)

We sail under the skin
in narrow tributaries
toward the open ocean
huge, frightening and unrhymed.

The Muse

It is early morning
The trees keep their watch
You know she is waiting
And you enter the forest
At first you do not see her
Then she is there
She takes your breath away
And grinds your bones to fine dust
You cannot stand
You lay your loins against the earth
and beg for entrance
This time she denies you
And her pride and distance anger you.
But you know you will do anything she asks.
She tells you to rise and walk
out of the forest.
You do (longing is in every step)
tomorrow you will enter
again
And before long she will make
You weep.
You will claim you love her
She will laugh
You will put down your pride
for her
And she will dance on it
You will offer her your life
And she will mock you.
But one day you will return
            bearing the
right gift
She will at last embrace
you, and you will speak.

No Place to Say

sealed
among the debris of the past
eggshell skies
and grey conversations,
sadness becomes a
waking thing
with no place to say
(following me through the day)

When One Can't Speak

Trapped words turn to fists
Words lodge in corners
claiming squatter's rights
Or hitchhike around the brain
Endlessly looking for a way out

Visiting Mr. Emerson's House at Concord

His spirit
made transparent
by intelligence
was sitting
as ever
spooning rich conversation
like New England autumn
into his mouth
I planned
to sit
by the fire
and listen
to my soul's content
to that craftsman
who shaped my thought
But ladies formal
with preservation
said in voices
stiff with concern,

"Move on, please"

Four haiku

Melting snow
I take a bath
Linking my heart to the sky.

sometimes we polish up our faces
and go out smiling like the moon
laughing to be in such fine company

first snow
listen!
the sunflowers stand mute.

The cat wakes up
startled
He must have heard himself dreaming.

A Poem to Greg Brown

I wanted to give you something
But my words do not come easily
And are as stiff as the father of the bride.
Maybe I could have given you the dime
I found while we were walking
But it doesn't buy much
And anyway it's no sacrifice
I did give you something in silence
My pledge of friendship,
But I wanted some words to
Frame, in some sense to prove
I am a poet,
But there is no proof in that.
Accept then the effort in these
Thoughts as concrete
As a June day and smiling
Like a midnight sun
And as cool as saying
You look like a jazz musician
When really you remind me of
A shy small-town boy
Who has always been a poet.

To Poet's Children

for Ada

All life is poetry
Though some is turned
Inside out
And the blood shows
Gently phosphorescent
Like a rose.

Ridicule

Last night the silence
swallowed me
Turn slowly
face it
walk deeper
deeper into it
Listen
invite it
to speak

It spoke in its
huge-jawed silence
and I could not breathe
for the weight of it.

Tangled in the Sky

I was too often tangled in the lure of freedom
Thinking that the blue sky meant what it said.

The cafeteria sign said
"There is no such thing as free lunch"

I looked in my pockets
I'd given all my change to the river

So I sold my integrity
And landed in the lap of my father
Who said: "Now I'll tell you what to do."

I had to listen.
It was years before I wrote a poem.

The Forming of a Poet

real winter
blowing through one like a
wide awake star
cleaning the mind
of its warm weather rumblings

glasses of sherry on
winter afternoons -
inviting the fog to settle in
clearing it out with
strongly brewed coffee.
Sharing young resiliency
with age's rigidity -
tempering
carefully grooming quotations
eating small sandwiches

CONTEMPLATION

Mary was a spiritual person who practiced yoga, meditation, and prayer. Her journals are full of quotes from religious and philosophical writings.

* A Moment

A moment is a shell upon the shore.
A crack in the wall.
The sound of a door closing.
The speed of light
The drop of water in the ocean
The dropping of a nickel in a parking meter
A stroke of paint
A minute full of lead
Ice
Fire
An hour full of humility
A gunshot
A flap of wings

The dropping of an egg
In the final transforming end
The clock will not be there

Make Straight the Way of the Lord

I have paused too often on this road
My curiosity's a dumb and dusty thing
And my eyes are clouded over.

I have spent too long
Smiling at the moon
And now my tongue can
Waggle only superstition,

I have studied the spiders' ways
And now my time is tangled
In their webs.
I have been too long
Meandering.   I must

Take off my shoes
And teach my feet

To pray.

Prayer

May the Lord
Find you
Sitting high
On a desert peak
With your eyes closed
Calling His name;

Ah ieeea Yaweh

And gently touch you
And open your eyes.
And may you walk
Down the mountain
Wrapt in love
Your moccasins
Barely touching the ground.

Ah ieeea the power of God

For I love you
Brother fox / salmon
My love touches you
As the sun

Accept my prayer
As you accept the wind.

Architects of the Universe ...

Architects of the Universe
Why look for blueprints
When you have the house?

Shall I hit the fly ...

Shall I hit the fly with my
HANDBOOK TO HIGHER CONSCIOUSNESS?

Old Poem

desire, pride, illusion, fear
    coat my wings

Being dreamers ...

Being dreamers we are likely
to get in over our
heads, then teach ourselves
to swim

I sense salvation in grey men ...

I sense salvation in grey men - reeking of loneliness, exuding it like decaying, yellowing manuscripts tucked away in hollow libraries - I enter grey old men like sunlight running its fingers on November corn and brushing it with admiration. I take blue skies with seasonal clouds into my eyes, now bluer with wisps of white. I listen to laughter, created out of worldly materials and made shimmering by love. I let music enter my ears and paint its myriad worlds and teach my voice to harmonize. I do all this to take to grey men who let boredom enter and do not demand it to leave, becoming it their bedfellow, draining them of color. I am not afraid - my world is full of low autumn sun glancing its golden eyes on its harvest and saying a farewell.

I have the dusky twilight settled in my heart from solitary wanderings and know its secrets. I have friends' full footsteps resounding, interweaving with sleepers' breathing and lovers' alternate quarreling and harmonizing - I have sounds that fill the house with individual worlds touched, embraced or rebuffed, bringing cold winds on flushed cheeks to meet warm hearth fires. These things I most willingly give. I have earth in my bones and vast silences that speak of peace not boredom.

Second Week Alone, Tucson Desert

despised solitude
beloved solitude
    times are
I sink compliantly
        into your silent arms

i raise havoc
with bitterness
and watch selfish
melodramas in
the private screening
room of my mind.
        or
rage, pounding my
eyes against these
obdurate walls
    white
pages stare blankly
at me as i force a dialogue
i spend hours watching
the honey drop into
my spoon
      ritual tea - again & again

> > >

i once knew solitude
of a more bitter kind.
Now, it is only i
among the noisy silences
of this room.

Though i suspect some
guardian angel stands
in that corner
and lends me light
when i can no longer see.

"The monkey is reaching for the moon ..."

"The monkey is reaching for the moon in the water / Even reaching death it would not give up / If only it would let go / and disappear into the deep pool / All directions would shine with / dazzling brightness."

Japanese story, quoted in Mary's journal

I am still the monkey on the branch, unwilling to let go - but always grasping after the reflection in the water. When I let go - the world will be dazzled by my purity - that is the promise of the KOAN

Come with me . . .

Come with me and tell
me the stories you know
about the stars
Tell me what you've heard the
wind say
and say it again

Dark envelope of sleep

Dark envelope of sleep
without it
I would confess everything.

old woman

passing days,
scaling off like
dried fish skin
mandarin nails
hardened   sinister
she sits
conversing with spirits

* Things move so fast ...

Things move so fast.
An image
In a second
and you
see the TV ads
and wonder who you are
(what's your star)

When times were
slower
you only knew
yourself, your friends.

And now
within a second
a million images send
to your brain
a million
Questions of who you might be.

Jehovah Witness Visit

Salesman of God
mindlessly repeating (Are you in league with Satan?)

blackbooked words in loud
voice
dull eyes closed ears do not
sparkle
    brotherhood
        claiming only one way

God is sharing, salesman, not
selling!

Source

Yes, and i said
    to him,
"According to what source?"
And he answered, "God"
And i in my ignorance
asked, "Who?"

Planning My Escape I

I rub my legs together like two
Sticks trying to start a fire.
But like the good girl scout that I am
I do not tell my mother.

I want out.

But I want no blood spilled,
Pain embarrasses me.

I send my eyes
They come back veiled.

I send my ears
They come excited about
The melodies they heard.

So they will not lose faith
I tell them the enemy is always
Trying to jam the lines.

I teach my fingers how to speak
So my tongue will not betray me,

But they have a mind of their own
And I have to keep them behind my back.

Down on my knees

I read all the maps.

I want out.   I must be firm.
In this lifetime.

Planning My Escape II

I finger the means of my escape
In one hand a prayer, in the other a poem.

One day I found a note, "You are starving,"
It said. Then I realized my hunger

And knew myself to be a prisoner.

It is not that my jailer is unkind
He gives me anything I want
Says I am free to stay or go.

He is subtle beyond words
Even now he is planning
To make me look ridiculous
Saying I wrote these plans

To impress the world,
Not because I desire to get out.

I sit silently, fingering the means
Of my escape;
In one hand a prayer, in the other a poem.

Planning My Escape III

My head was full of escape I
Was looking for a plan
When I

Met a lady
Sweetly ironing
The morning air I

Asked her nothing.

There was a crow
Without legs
Before I

Could feel sorry
For him
He taught me how to dance.

A man selling roses
Advised me to sit down
But the crow was still

Dancing in my head.

Twilight was gathering
For some sweet feast I
Asked if I could stay

> > >

A beggar stirring
Rag soup didn't say I
Admired the diamonds

Beginning to appear He
Asked if I were a stranger here I
Said, "A toast to men who are not dancing bears." He

Filled his hat with soup and handed it to me.

It reminded me of hunger just
Then jugglers appeared
And juggled thin air for free.   I

Asked about escape.   A road appeared.
That was the last I
Saw of myself.

it is noon ...

it is noon
and I have lit a fire
in the stove to chase
the grey chill away.
The afternoon is uncharted
before me
I wish to sink like a stone
into the heart of what matters.

The baby and Cosmo ...

The baby and Cosmo,
the fire, the music and I —
on a rainy Thursday afternoon
Who would not recognize this as perfection
has missed a great beauty.

Making Puppets
   or the art of healing

A little girl wanted to make a puppet
Of Jesus
She brought silence to us all
We convinced her to make a bunny.
Young men made horses that everyone admired.
An evangelist made one
And taught him
How to preach.
Two women worked all day and when they
Were done had the look of Geppetto
Hopeful of magic transformation.
A mother of four made five
Then washed all the scissors
and the room took on the feeling
of the first day of creation.

It was the ancient healing
making images with ourselves.

Chanting for My God

I sit listening to great
Thunderstorms
sifting dark soil
through my fingers
squat like a native
I am silent
like all great pools of water.
I wish only to sink
like a stone.
Others move around me
We do not make connections
And I am lonely
for them
But continue chanting for
my God.

A Conversation

there is an uncommon silence here
a sense of drifting
i feed on cricket sounds
and limit my understanding.

spirits become angry with me
and threaten to put cotton stuffing
in my brain.

I say nothing to fistfuls of stars
and piss on my shoelaces again,
I swear I will be more conscious next time.

and you know what I'm going to say;
the world is full of abandoned hearts
and the wounded who do not bleed.

* Bizzy

Patients to wash
and beds to change
hands attached
to a clumsy brain.

Quickly hands learn your duties
so the brain can drift
to other things.

* Why I Was Late

I was trying to write
this late rich light
of Autumn
burning every bush like Moses's
eyes the afternoon he saw fully.
Dry corn is restless,
like an entire continent of people.
Forgive me if I am late.
I could not move in this afternoon prayer.
It seemed irreverent.
Now it dulls a little.
I will move on.
The wind sounds like
something coming.
I turn around to see
it is only winter.

Mortality

Mary spent a lot of time with her older friends and with people in nursing homes. I think those experiences added to her interest in mortality, an interest that seems ironic in retrospect considering her death at a relatively young age.

Death in the Iowa Winter

-To Immanuel

There is a frozen goat
Hanging in the woodshed.

The child asks:

"Will you put it in the
Ground next spring?"

His mother answers: "yes."

"Will it grow like the
Seeds we plant?"

His mother answers: "no."

I sense shadows
Crossing his mind.

Self-portrait

I paint a self-portrait
And present it to the world
I hope they will accept it;
It is a striking likeness.

I am preoccupied
With the impression I am making
Taking careful note of reactions,
Watching facial expressions
And paying attention
To the tone of all replies,

Weighing respect by how much
Interest is displayed.

An intense preoccupation.

I step outside.

The sidewalk screams I am a coward
I grind my shoe into its cracked grin
And lose my sock

Something strange enters my blood
And I howl at the moon.

> > >

Carnival mirrors of self
Hysterical
Explode
A million slivers of glass
All come through the skin

Making me a delicate porcupine.

Walking by mirrors now
There is no reflection.

I am obviously a ghost.

And what is it for a ghost to be afraid?

Jock

Jock died yesterday
    Jock
My friend, one who found in me what others find -
    and I see not -
Jock is dead at 23
    We talked about bicycling in Europe in the fall
    I tried to cajole him into taking me /
    or at least thinking about it.
He is gone
    Such a strange thing - death so close -
    tapping on the door.
I try to think of death at 23
I try to think of Jock
I think of him constantly - and yet
I do not know what to think
    Only that he is on my mind.
Perhaps I think of him here / not here
    Or greater yet
I think of death as such a huge force - power -
Nothing is recalled from it -
    no matter how contrite or what bargaining you do -
    It is not reversible
Such a mystery - a huge depth - this person,
Never to be seen on earth again in his familiar form,
    What it does to the family who knew him
    as part of their whole
    And now a part is missing
    A gap
    An empty space which was once filled
    with a living breathing flesh -
    Now - - space /

    > > >

We keep repeating the event
as if to unravel
the awesome mystery
to somehow tell enough
(perhaps we've missed some detail)
to change the ending
that irrevocable clang

Death, you put on some show.

Jock II

That boy, he
went in a bicycle race
simply got off his bike
and died -
no time for illness
or thought
on a clear blue day
racing like the wind
until becoming it.

A Small Poem for Ralph

I was driving
The sun was traveling
As delicate as ever
And I thought about
How they go
Leaving huge white spaces
That remind us of silence

Loudness beats in our hearts
And we could go right off the road.

* Nursing Home Visit

I come suntanned from the country
bringing fresh eyes
to the stale unchanging, but for
death's ever nearer presence,
corridors
eyes clouded with
memories
staring blankly at
my fresh air eyes
And do not know me.

I drive away back into
blue skies and long roads
admonishing myself to use
my journey well
and to always be thankful
for the gift of fresh air
and clear eyes.
And to keep before me the memory
of those souls waiting for release.

Father William

a story told in Whiting, Iowa

It was March
Yes, March
Father wasn't feeling well
His body ran fevers like spring
and he feared something he couldn't tell

I gave hot camphor for comfort
and rubbed his stiff legs down
It was the last I'd see of Father
for that night he drown

The day was cold as steel and hard
but he took his gunny sacks
and went to seed his celery beds
Ah, Father feared something he didn't know

Our cousins walked home near the lake that night
"Look," said one, "a duck"
      "Hush," said the other, "it's Uncle William"

Our dinner was laughing and gay
until the news came
"Your father, he's drown"

> > >

    His sacks lay by his side
    death held his hand
        bony and cold
And the food turned March grey
It was too dark to go that night
so we left him in the
arms of March ice
all of us dreaming of drowning

    Poor Father he's gone
    he's drown
he feared what he didn't know

Auction

    Guts of houses
        spilled out on the lawn

A lifetime
    up for sale
    handled and bought
        by strangers
            to be someday sold again
       is there agony in the
people
       Spilled all over the lawn,
    or are they beyond possessing?

Miss Brooks - 1977

Perched like a bird on her cage
Quick black eyes dart,
And hands flutter like August butterflies.

She's been here since 1952
And is still a newcomer;

"People in small towns are slow
To make friends."

She keeps an old ivory teething ring,
Locks of hair from children
Who died of diphtheria and
A pearl found by her mother
In the oyster stew.

Even the sunbeams are dusty.

Working at the Cafe

Bacon sizzles like rain,
Onions peel like lives

And Connie Francis sings:
"Be Anything But Be Mine."

Rolls lie entombed in glass
Waiting for rows of cemetery teeth,

And greased fingers slide off dreams
Like eggs off the griddle.

The place is littered with bones
I pick them up gingerly
And wash them of their sins

I say little
And pour the black libations
They toast to weary hands

Cradles to Death

I

Handling human bodies
    old human bodies
        dying human bodies
           (seeing the bones through the skin)
    bathing them
        and cleaning their excrement
dressing
    them like big dolls.

II

I dropped Agatha Mason on the bathroom floor
    today

    She just lay
        there
           screaming
    "My leg, my leg," an immovable heap
I just stood there,
    my heart fled
    looking at that screaming
heap of humanity -
    i dropped Agatha Mason on
the floor today
    i felt very small

III

I hate to go to work tomorrow
The days are a little harder to endure -
    Work is dropping Agatha on the floor
    Running errands
    Listening to constant bitching

        "don't let him go in that bathroom,
        then he'll go there all the time &
        we who can't use the other bathroom
        will suffer...."

And the nurse is mad at an aide
And we all work too hard & no thanks for
Cleaning shit -
        & no wonder
that nerves get frazzled & bared
      ready to snap
          no wonder
              there are so few kind
                  words
              so little time for
              kindnesses when you
              have so much to do.

                    > > >

IV

Her husband died last year
    (and she sleeps alone)
Her sons are married and gone
    (and she eats alone)
Her co-workers don't listen to her
    (and she speaks alone)
I have been unkind, she speaks
    of loneliness ...
        And i
        who eat and sleep with many
        refused to listen.

V

minds
    traveling to
        pasts to futures
        to nowhere?
like birds'
    claws clinging to
footrests
    and sheets,
        cradles to death

VI

And one died today -
as Mrs. O'Donnell put it, it was a rare opportunity to
observe death;
it doesn't often accommodate her in her training program
(but i am too harsh on her -
she is, she will be one of them ...
and her nights must be long)

The dead one looked as she did in life, dying.
Then the sheet
Then she was much more frightening and mysterious
Death under a sheet has a strong effect

Did a soul fly out and ascend?

Someone asked me to pray for her.
I must try to remember names.

> > >

VII — Faith
to Mattie

She sat in her chair
   for a week
      in her
         own
           excrement … praying …
And they found her
    and brought her here
    And she thanks you every day
    for saving her and being so kind,
        And she tells you
    how lucky she is …

            She is mocked
      and abused but she
    looks for a Christian in
    everyone's eyes.
  Keep her, oh Lord.

VIII

bus riding
  snow falling
    so silently
  people dying
    so noisily
what if we could
      fall as silently and gently as snow?

IX

At the nursing home
They sit
The lady says
Sing now / row / row / row
Your boat - move
Your hands -

Hands flutter like
feeble birds
and I think
so it comes to this....

X

She stared straight ahead; outside the sun was shining. The air was crystal - one of those frozen winter days that could easily break you into tiny frozen pieces.

She stared, aware of the frozenness outside, but had long forgotten the feel of cold air on skin and the relaxing relief of warmth. Inside, a chill might vibrate through the air, but never the frozen fingers of winter. The view out her window might as well have been a painting: it was not alive; as unchanging as the temperature.

She wondered what it was she had forgotten; she could never remember. Had she left her gloves on the train; had she forgotten to order the necessary things? She only knew somewhere she had forgotten it all.

> > >

She knew time passed, though she had forgotten what it was; somehow she slept, was awakened and slept again. She sat; next to her only refuge, her bed. It was also her friend; it asked nothing of her but to forget; it never asked her to try to remember. It never tired her out like the sitting and standing and bathing.

She longed for the blackness, the gentle solace of sleep, though she never spoke of the word, or even remembered it as dying. The daylight hours were harsh, demanding that she sit up, eat, go to the bathroom, take a bath and try to remember. She was afraid for she did remember one thing: the space; the terrible loneliness that filled that space like a vacuum. She quickly tried to forget; she took shelter in her bed.

What was left, what remained? She wouldn't think of that. She wouldn't think of that. Every day she would sit and stare straight ahead and try desperately to forget what she couldn't remember.

She felt the air was stale, and smelled of urine, but she had forgotten fresh air, so she accepted it even though she often dreamed of suffocating.

She lived on the fourth floor; in a city. She knew she had lived in a different, better place before. If she thought about it, if she were aware of it, she knew her brain would scream and scream, the sound floating down an empty tunnel.

Voices and hands broke her monotony, to lift, or give directions, or tire her, but they came quickly and were gone as flashes of sun on a lake and forgotten in the darkening pool of old age. She wished that her mind could be like the others' who sat all day in worlds far from here, worlds of odd phrases and no sight, in their death wait cut off from . . . They alone knew where they were as they spoke of old things, like putting out bits and pieces of old string. They never suffered, the lucky ones. Time passed.

But she still remembered. She knew she was no longer useful; she knew she was a burden, a weight a stone forever sinking, and that time was as crippled as she. But what was she supposed to remember,

Oh what:
remembering, whispering, remember
all the good times melting like ice cream
in July down the front of your dress & the
Caresses and satisfactions remembering remember
like the moon in the early morning sun disappearing
like disintegrating tissue
Remembering remember when legs were young
and supple like a young colt's . . . what was it . . .
yes . . .what . . was . . that . . feeling . .
what was that feeling, Ah the sun on skin, the
Sun . . . not imposed on a window
but, melting ice cream down the front of a
summer, oh i'm so tired i can't remember anymore
gone gone remember remembering gone gone all
gone put me to bed please, i'm tired . . . i'm
so tired
ohdearohdearohdearohdearohdear

Clothes

I can communicate some with my
clothes
much more with my skin
(and the skin will tell its lie)
a world with my heart
and beyond that the soul —
the glove of God's most merciful hand —
carried on its beautiful love affair
with death in whispers i barely hear.

Restaurant

Grandma's tired
She's got no place to go
so she falls asleep with
the TV on, in the room
      where Pa stayed
           before he
                went away

To My Grandmother, Dying During a Snowstorm

Around the house I circle
My grandmother dies
Snowflake by snowflake
As we all fall down
All fall down.

Snow, sounding like death
Falls on the roof of my grandmother's.

My grandmother's tomb
Whispering memories that
Even outside, hear in
The softness, hear in
The silence.

Trees bowed like beggars
Burdens of snow,
Burdens of death.

I say I will not forget
The soft silent circling of death

And the terrible beauty of
Your dying.

The Gift

He sat in his room
and thought about space.
It grows smaller he thought.
Once it was the world,
then a room
and now a bed
and soon the size of a coffin.

He thought of all the gifts he had been given.
Some not acknowledged,
some glossed over in carelessness,
some neglected, some treasured and kept.
As he thought about all that he had received,
he wondered what he might return.

He would carve ebony birds,
graceful and black as an African evening.
So he did and sent them out.
Once he sent a dollar to a girl
in Japan, lonely for home and the
light of love.

I never forgot the gift
And it has given me cause to think of
all the gifts I have been given.
To Pop Nickoley I give the gift
of remembrance.
May his flight be graceful as the birds.

Weaving

Weaving
We are weaving our shrouds
The days
They are threads
That we are weaving
We are weaving our shrouds
Our Father
Has warped the loom
But we are the weavers
No day is dropped from the loom
No hour
No minute
They all go into the weaving
We are weaving
We are weaving our shrouds
There is only rest at night
All the rest is weaving
Every thought
Every breath
in and out
of the warp
Weaving
We are weaving
We are weaving our shrouds
When the master
At last
Cuts the threads
We will see the pattern
We have woven
We are the weavers
Weaving our shroud
And it will be the only thing
We have to wear to our grave.

Acknowledgments

A grateful thank you to those who made this book possible:

Greg Brown for his touching Foreword;

Lucy Hanson Homstad and Joseph Paul Homstad for putting together the poems in the first book, *Weavings;*

Andrea Austin Homstad for transcribing the poems from *Weavings;*

James Nels Homstad and Homstad Farm for financial support;

Corby and Nick Preus for help with editing;

Phyllis Price for proofreading; and

Eric Hustvedt of Talent Bank Communications for assembling the book for publication.

Carl Homstad
Springwater Road Publishing

About the Author

Mary Jo Homstad was born on March 21, 1947. She died in an automobile accident on December 1, 1978 at the age of 31. The daughter of Dr. Joseph Homstad and Lucy Hanson Homstad, Mary grew up in Denver Colorado. In 1965 she enrolled at Luther College, Decorah, Iowa, where she received a BA in English in 1969. After graduation she spent a year teaching English in Japan. She lived in rural Decorah.

Mary had many jobs, but she always saw herself as a poet. She would fill small notebooks with thoughts, phrases, overheard dialogue, drafts of poems and quotations from her favorite writers. When she had accumulated several notebooks, she would transcribe and revise the thoughts and poems into a large hardbound volume. She had created several of these volumes when she died.

In 1980 her mother Lucy, with the help of Mary's brother Joe and editor Douglas Anderson, put together a book of poems and drawings from Mary's journals called *Weavings*. The first print run of 600 copies led to a second printing. She also had poems in various publications.

www.ingramcontent.com/pod-product-compliance
Lightning Source LLC
Chambersburg PA
CBHW021954290426
44108CB00012B/1071